The Way Home

A spoken word opera

by

Constance Alexander

Finishing Line Press
Georgetown, Kentucky

The Way Home

A spoken word opera

Dedicated to Marcia, Kay, Pat, Kathy, & Teresa

Copyright © 2020 by Constance Alexander
ISBN 978-1-64662-345-7 First Edition
All rights reserved under International and Pan-American Copyright Conventions. No part of this book may be reproduced in any manner whatsoever without written permission from the publisher, except in the case of brief quotations embodied in critical articles and reviews.

Royalties: There are no royalty payments required for presenting *The Way Home*, but producing organizations are asked to:

- Contact the playwright when performances are scheduled.

- Donate proceeds from performances to non-profit organizations related to the themes explored in *The Way Home*.

- Send copies of all promotional materials associated with productions to the playwright, to document where the piece is performed and what causes its proceeds have supported. This requirement is in lieu of royalties to the playwright.

- Follow appropriate copyright laws, and purchase cast and director copies of *The Way Home* for performances through www.finishingline press.com

Publisher: Leah Huete de Maines
Editor: Christen Kincaid
Cover Art: Stephen Leonardi at Unsplash.com
Author Photo: Robyn Pizzo, www.robynpizzo.com
Cover Design: Andrew Davis at adada.com

Order online: www.finishinglinepress.com
also available on amazon.com

Author inquiries and mail orders:
Finishing Line Press
P. O. Box 1626
Georgetown, Kentucky 40324
U. S. A.

Background Notes: *The Way Home* was inspired by two-and-a-half years of interviews with more than sixty people about end-of-life issues for a series of print articles and a documentary radio series with WKMS-FM, the National Public Radio affiliate in Murray, Ky. The script weaves together the stories of two characters, Pat and Theresa, and incorporates threads from many other interviews conducted for the project.

Definitions: The term "spoken word opera" seems apt for the material, as the work reflects many of the qualities of an opera—arias, duets, a chorus—but it is meant to be spoken. Designed as readers' theatre, it is to be read rather than memorized, thus allowing performances by actors with a range of abilities and a span of ages. The focus is on the text and the voices, not on sets, blocking, costumes, or props.

Technical Flexibility: *The Way Home* is easily performed in theatre and non-theatre settings, including community rooms, places of worship, school auditoriums, libraries, medical and nursing schools, senior citizen housing, and—of course—professional, community, and university theaters. Any place where people might gather to talk about end-of-life issues is suitable, and directors' uses of lighting, blocking, special effects, etc. often enhance the spoken words.

Community Partnerships: Groups presenting *The Way Home* are encouraged to establish partnerships with local or regional groups such as Relay for Life, hospice, American Cancer Society, etc., so they can work together to distribute appropriate literature in conjunction with performances. In addition, directors might consider selecting a local or regional media person to take the part of the Reporter, as that would help in promoting *The Way Home*. Whoever is cast, performances are intended to stimulate discussion and spark civic action so that communities, institutions, and individuals are better able to provide much-needed support for those struggling with cancer, terminal illness, or the emotional and financial challenges associated with the end of life.

Production History: Horse Cave Theatre featured a reading of the script in April, 2003, as part of its Kentucky Voices series. In 2003, a revised version was featured at the West Kentucky Playwrights' Festival, and *The Way Home* was the centerpiece of the 2003 national conference of the Association of Joint Labor-Management Educational Programs at the Roosevelt Hotel in New York. In 2013, an excerpt was featured in *Scenes from the Common Wealth*, published by MotesBooks.

The Way Home has been performed at various locations in Kentucky, as well as in New York City, New Jersey, Louisiana, New York State, Illinois, California, Georgia, and Arkansas. Readings are scheduled throughout the year, but often in October, for Breast Cancer Awareness Month, or November, National Hospice Month. All performances have raised funds for causes related to women's health, breast cancer, hospice, and the uninsured, often in conjunction with organizations such as Susan Komen Foundation, Gilda's Club, or Relay for Life.

Grants & Awards: Grants and support from Kentucky Foundation for Women, the Kaiser Foundation, Kentucky Arts Council, the Pilgrim Project and the Ragdale Foundation contributed to the development of *The Way Home*. Ms. Alexander is an award-winning newspaper columnist, poet, playwright, and fiction writer. She has five published books of poetry to her credit, as well as a memoir. A founding member of the West Kentucky Playwrights Festival, she has written numerous plays, all of which have production histories in professional, university, and community theatres.

Characters:

Reporter*—Middle-aged woman, working on a documentary series about death and dying.

Theresa—Woman in her early 50's, fighting cancer for the third time. Cannot afford health insurance because of her pre-existing condition.

Pat—Widow in her late 60's, suffering from Parkinson's Disease and recently diagnosed with Stage IV breast cancer.

Chorus—Two or three females, director's choice on ages.

*When possible, a female media personality should be enlisted for the part of Reporter. That way, readings of *The Way Home* may attract larger audiences and warrant more extensive media coverage.

Table of Contents:

Act I	Show Me the Way	Page 4
Act II	Looking Up	Page 13
Act III	Things Fall Apart	Page 21
Act IV	The Other Shoe	Page 29
Act V	Otherwise	Page 35

Act I—Show Me the Way

CHORUS

Theresa Flowers
Trigg County (east of the lake)
Breast, 37
Ovarian, 50
No insurance
Donaldson Creek Road—half-mile from church
Turquoise trailer, look for mailbox

THERESA

Turn right,
right after the lake.
Follow that road.

REPORTER

Past junked cars,
rusted-out school buses,
a quarry, the sign
for an old church
that burned down.

THERESA

When you get to the creek,
turn left.
You're there when you get
to the mailbox with flowers
on it.

Right here.

REPORTER

Let's see.
Tape recorder.
Batteries.
Notebook.
Pen. Not that one.
I've got to get
a better notebook.
Not today.

THERESA

I've been listening for you.
For the car.

REPORTER
Your directions were great.
Didn't get lost once but
I never actually saw the quarry.

CHORUS
She stands on the porch of her trailer;
hugs herself against the chill.
The scarf wrapped around her head is splashed
with purple, fuchsia and rivers
of green. Her hands flutter to straighten
the scarf, to check the swell of its silken knot
and the tucked-in tails.

THERESA
I washed my hair today and a lot of it fell out.
When I came outside to dry my head off,
the rest of it went.

CHORUS
The autumn colors have faded to rust.
The sedge grass is bleached blond.

THERESA
The leaves are falling and my hair's falling out.
So I thought, well, that's ok. In the spring,
the leaves will all come back
and so will my hair.
It's kind of like that. Life's
like that sometimes.
Come on in.
We'll sit here.

CHORUS
Afternoon sun slants through the lace curtains.
On the kitchen table a bowl of plums,
sleek purple orbs, smooth as gigolos.
The cloth, handmade, is from Budapest,
embroidered with blue and white flowers.

THERESA
I need pretty things around me.
I'm an artist.

REPORTER
My favorite color. Blue.
Hmmm. What smells so good?

THERESA
I made tea and baked muffins.
The smell of the muffins reminds me that
I want my mother. Not my real mother
but the mother I wish I had,
who could keep me safe
and read me stories until
I fall asleep.
I can feel her hand gentle and cool on my forehead,
checking for fever.

REPORTER
Good. Well. Right? How nice.
Did you know there's a greater than 1 in 10 chance
a woman will contract breast cancer
some time in her lifetime?
Over 1 million women find lumps in their breasts
each year.

CHORUS
Well, that was stupid, wasn't it?
And she hasn't even gotten to
ovarian yet. Will there be more statistics?
What did she do with that list?

THERESA
I'm one in a million.
I was thirty-seven.
Never even had a cold.
My partner and I didn't have health insurance.
We couldn't afford it.
We were starving artists.
The payments would have been $550 a month
for the two of us.
We decided we'd think about health insurance
when we were forty.

CHORUS
Forty. Probably
seemed a million
years away.

THERESA
I've always been the kind of person
who pays for everything.
Never even had a credit card.
I thought, if you don't have the money,

you just do without.

But then the lump.

After the surgery there were bills.
Hospital, doctors, drug companies for the chemo,
labs. I sold my house to pay them off,
but at least my life was free and clear,
and I was free and clear.

I even got an IRA.
Bought myself a future.

But not health insurance.
No one would sell it to me.

REPORTER

Too much of a risk?

THERESA

Too much of a risk.

CHORUS

Pages on a calendar
in an old movie,
like shuffling a deck of cards.
Thirteen years pass that fast.
A candle burns down to the nub.
The bright red pick-up succumbs to rust.
Every six months there are tests
and every one of them says it's ok
until that one.

THERESA

They hoped it was a false reading
but it wasn't.
This time - ovarian.
Attached itself to my bowel.
A mess.
Full hysterectomy and a lot
of extra stuff.
They started chemotherapy three weeks
after the surgery.

CHORUS

You wait 'til they call your name
at the Four Rivers

Cancer Center.
The chairs are lined up like a firing squad.
Stiff, gray plastic.
A Coke machine hums its single note
until someone actually buys one.
One, two, three, four
quarters and then the thud of the can
dropping. It could be a gunshot,
the way we all jump.

These are the rules:
One
Wait until your name is called.
Two
The uninsured
must pay on demand.
Three
Co-pays and deductibles
are due at time of service.

These are the magazines:
Golf Digest.
Farm Wife.
Art and Antiques.
Popular Mechanics.
Only one issue of *Time*.
Of course. The one
we need more of.

REPORTER
So what's it like? Chemotherapy.

THERESA
You have to take steroids and
Tagamet before.
It makes your bones hurt
but they say it's good for you.

When they call you, it's time
to go into the room.
There's a whole bunch of people together.
Hooked up to tubes.

REPORTER
A group? You're not alone?
I'd hate that.

THERESA
We sit in a circle like Girl Scouts.
We talk a lot because of the steroids
we take the night before.

CHORUS

I couldn't sleep at all.

So what did you do?

Worked in the shop making birdhouses.

Needlework.

Listened to the radio.

Me too.

Classical.

Oldies.

Jazz.

THERESA
When I'm really bad, I like country
and western. It makes me laugh.

REPORTER
Someone should write a country song about chemo.

CHORUS
No one told me your pubic hair falls out.

No more bikini waxes.

I have to draw on eyebrows.

False eyelashes.

It always gets down to hair.

Falling out.

Hair. That's a big one.

Can I borrow your hat?
I'm bald as a bat.

THERESA
It's hard on my veins.
Chemo. They collapse.
I've lost a couple already.
It's easier when you have a port.

REPORTER
A port?

THERESA
Something that's put into your chest
so you don't need an IV.

It means more surgery
and I don't want more surgery.

And it's the expense.
Since I'm paying out of pocket
I'll forego a port until
I really need one.

CHORUS
Chemo's hell on the veins,
so at some point
you have to have a port.

Always a port in a storm.

THERESA
A girl in my group has had some kind of cancer,
and disfiguring surgery. Part of her chin's
gone. She can't talk or eat. She's fed
through a tube in her stomach.

She writes questions in a big spiral notebook
and you answer them out loud.
She can hear. She just can't talk.

She told me she goes through four or five
of those notebooks a week.

    (As if talking to the girl with the notebook.)
You must talk an awful lot.

We got to be good friends.
She's just such a beautiful person.
She was awfully upset about losing her hair.
I thought, my goodness, this girl has been through so much
and she's upset about her hair.

With everything else, I'll be more disfigured.

You can wear pretty scarves, a cute hat.

Sure. I'll show you how to wrap your head.

Put on a pair of sun glasses and they'll think
you're a movie star.

You wear your hat or your scarf
or your wig. Or even go bald-headed.
After awhile it just becomes part of who you are
and people don't see it anymore.

   (As if reading what the girl with the notebook wrote.)
Honest?

Honest.

You have a beautiful soul.
It shows in your eyes.
Nobody even notices things like hair
when they can see what's in your heart and soul.
Look at the way you've handled your life.
You're radiant.
Courage like that is beautiful.

CHORUS
But we still cry when our hair falls out.
No matter what.

THERESA
Only thing I can read
during chemo
is Louis L'Amour.
I love the cheap hotels, the gun fights,
a new marshal comes to town to kick butt.

CHORUS
Utah Blaine. El Paso.

I come to rout this town
of the varmint that's stealing horses
and robbin' banks.

It ain't right. Losing three marshals
in three months.

I stopped cattle rustlin' up north,
train robberies out west.
You think I can't clean up this town?

His spurs make as much noise as tap dancer shoes,
but he's no sissy, even tho' he tips his hat
to the ladies and says yes ma'am and no ma'am
like some mealy-mouth mama's boy.
He's rangy, raw-boned, squinty-eyed but not in a shifty way,
if ya know what I mean.

It's from riding into all them sunsets.

When he pushes the doors of the saloon open
the place gets all quiet like, and the bartender starts polishin'
clean glasses with a dirty towel and dartin' looks into the mirror.
The guys playin' poker push away from the table in back.
And the chorus girls sneak upstairs so they don't
get their feathers blown off in a gunfight or nothin'.
Utah's faster on the draw than the outlaw,
but he don't kill him. He takes him in and waits
for the judge to come to town 'cause that's the way justice works.

No lynchin' on my watch. We do things legal-like.
The hangin' judge'll be here 'fore the next new moon.

Act II—Looking Up

THERESA
Winter solstice.
The article's in
the paper today.
My birthday.
Fifty.
My garden sleeps
beneath violet shadows.
I light a candle
and hang the house
with evergreens
to keep the year alive.
The longest night,
the shortest day.
I have dreams.
I'm in tight places.
Underground.
I have to get to the other side.
Just when it seems I can't,
I do.

REPORTER
The first article about Theresa was printed in the paper December 21. On the 24th, a reader named Pat emailed. I don't know why I was even at the computer on Christmas Eve. I should've been wrapping presents or decking the halls but—

PAT
—I would like to send some money to help Theresa.
Is there a fund or can we start one?
I don't know how she can do it with no insurance.
I can give a thousand dollars to start.
Anonymously.

Her plight struck me immediately.
Medicare and supplemental insurance is all
that keeps me from being in the same spot.

I was first diagnosed with ovarian cancer last January.
Turned out it was breast cancer that had spread.
Doctors tell me I'm terminal.
I may last another year,
but I get hints I probably won't.
I take chemo every three weeks to maintain

some quality of life while I'm living.
I had physical check-ups, including mammograms
every year, but my cancer was detected too late.
I hope Theresa will overcome this once again.

Pat—*pc65@apex.net*

REPORTER

Dear Pat—
There is no fund for Theresa,
but I'll see what I can find out
about setting one up at the bank.
In the meantime,
I'd love to interview you.
You know from reading the paper
I'm doing this series
on end of life issues.
It sounds like you
have some wisdom to share.
What do you think?

PAT

If I can help Theresa,
that also helps me.
I sometimes wonder
if I have gone out of my way
to help anybody.
I have some,
but I think back and believe
I could have done more.
But then, hindsight
is sharper than foresight.

I don't know what kind of story I have to tell
but I'd be glad to talk to you.

Pat—*pc65@apex.net*

REPORTER

December 27.
1404 Cardinal Drive.
Off Doran Road.
New notebook. A Christmas
present. Batteries.
Two pens. Always carry an extra.
Where's my recorder?
She says she's had Parkinson's

for ten years. And now
cancer. I don't know how
to do this.

PAT

When I'm nervous
the tremors start.
My voice flutters
like it's trapped
and trying to find
a way out.
I may be nervous during
the interview.

REPORTER

So nice to meet you.
Tea is fine.

CHORUS

This is what terminal cancer looks like?
Blue turban anchored with a purple scarf and a hat pin.
Eyes, deep lapis.

Silk blouse flocked
with color. Squares of
red, purple, blue, beige.
Necklace, a series of interlocking triangles.

The Christmas decorations are still up.
Tiny lights flicker
in the lenses of her glasses
as she passes a plate of cookies.
Cup rattles
against saucer.

PAT

I told you I'd be nervous.
Maybe I don't have anything to say.

REPORTER

Just tell me about yourself.

PAT

I've lived here 46 years.
It's definitely home.
I live alone now. My husband of 43 years
died 6 years ago.

We met in Texas
but I was born in
Kalamazoo.

Yes, I miss him. Even still.

We used to go fishing together.

CHORUS

Those days in favorite hollows,
sculling our craft
through inlet shallows.
You in the bow,
me in the aft.

You look for fish
and I,
line and color.
Together we bathe
in sunlight and shadow.

Your line flies out in a whisper,
seeking prey with a purr
and a buzz. Whoosh!
A fish cuts through the water
and fights to live another day.

Then all is silent
except for a muted choir of birds.
The fish we most admire
are feeding once again,
less the one in the hold.

Earth and sky lose their golden glow.
The sun is lost and sinking.
Evening slips into lavender,
leaving distant lights blinking.
The air lies heavy with dew.

Blend of earth and lake together
always remind me of you.

PAT

I miss him. Even now.

Family? That's what you asked,
isn't it?

Four.
Two boys, two girls.
They give me wonderful support.
And grandchildren.

Yes, I've given a lot of thought
to end of life decisions—
medically, financially, spiritually.
My children and I have talked about it.
I've started giving things away,
things I've treasured all my life.
And it's so easy. The giving.

No, I'm not always this
cheerful. I think about
the doctors who examined me
and said I was physically sound.

Yes, I did have a mammogram.
A couple of times.
There was a suspicious spot.

CHORUS

Come back in six months.

PAT

No one seemed
all that worried
but I did go back.
And they decided
nothing was there.

CHORUS

Come back in six months.

Come back in six months.

Well, maybe something.

You have a touch of
breast cancer, my dear.
Stage 4.
Should have gotten here
sooner.

PAT

Of course I think about the doctors,

but that kind of thinking gets me
nowhere. I have empathy too.
How do they feel?
Knowing they failed
to detect it?
I just concentrate on my treatments.

CHORUS
Chemo every three weeks,
blood tests in between.

PAT
I write down my questions
for the doctors
in a notebook just like yours,
but they choose their own time
to tell you things.
I don't know if it's because mine
is terminal, but they don't want
to answer my questions.
Maybe it bothers them
that I can't be fixed.
But if I can stand to ask,
why can't they answer?
I have to know things,
whether they're good or not.
I want to know how it's progressing,
or if the chemo is doing something.
Anything. I want to know.
But when I ask him questions—

CHORUS
Why are you asking so many questions?
You're not going to be tested on this.

REPORTER
What would you like to say to your doctor,
if you could get him to listen?

PAT
(Starts out mildly, but gets more aggressive.)
I would say: Because you aren't hearing that I want to know what's going on,
I'm having to read a lot of books and learn to speak your language.
I got a book on anatomy and physiology and started looking in the glossary
to find the words in my pathology report. And I spend time online. Looking
for information.

I don't know if everybody feels this way, but I've met a lot of women on the Internet like me. Now I don't like to get up in people's faces and say things they don't want to hear. I just want you to realize that I want to know what's going on. I have a right to know, don't I?

You're not going to write that in your article?

Well, maybe if you didn't use my last name.

CHORUS

She curls up in the chair,
and strokes the purple velvet
with her finger tips.
The tassels on the arms
slip through her fingers.
She sees him everywhere.
In the doorway, arms wrapped around
a basket of apples. In the bowl of irises
that sits on the sill. In the house they lived in once
with trellised roses and a cherry tree along the side.
They read the Sunday funnies together
and laugh.

She looks for him everywhere.
He is the only one she sees.

REPORTER

Pat—Please see attachment.
I hope the article's ok.
I didn't use your real name,
but anyone who knows you will know that it's you.
I wanted it to be informative and
to capture your spirit.
I did not want to get sappy or sentimental.
As it says in the first paragraph, you are many things—
a widow, a mother, grandmother, genealogist, amateur historian,
former member of the Women's Army Auxiliary Corps, a trained surgical technician, an artist, a photographer, a poet.
And a realist.

PAT

Thank you for sending
the article. I like that.
A realist.
I was a little nervous
about telling my story, but maybe
it will prompt others to seek medical help

sooner when they suspect something
is not right.

This is off the record,
but I thought you might like to know.
My oncologist seemed less in a hurry this time
and took some time for questions.
I asked about my tumor markers.
He looked through my file and found the information.
When I started chemo last June it was 170.
Today the reading was 19.
That's very good, by the way.
The nurse told me he read the article,
but he wouldn't let on to me.
So I asked my whole list of other questions.

Pat—*pc65@apex.net*

CHORUS
Why are you asking so many questions?
You're not going to be tested on this.

Act III—Things Fall Apart

THERESA
Now I'm getting two kinds of chemo.
At once.

CHORUS
One's company.
Two's a crowd.
Three's too many.
Four—

—Will probably kill you.

THERESA
My hands hurt.
They burn.
The creases and cracks
between every finger are so inflamed
I can't bend them or grip anything.
It's spreading to my feet,
though not as bad, and
I have a rash on both arms.

Gross, huh?

I can peel my hands like I'm husking corn.

CHORUS
(These warnings should be recited simultaneously.)

WARNING: Experience with high cumulative doses of Doxil is too limited to have established effects on the myocardium. Irreversible myocardial toxicity leading to congestive heart failure often unresponsive to cardiac supportive therapy may be encountered. Acute infusion-associated reactions—flushing, shortness of breath, facial swelling, headache, chills, back pain, tightness in throat or chest and/or hypotension—have occurred in about 5% to 10% of patients treated with Doxil.

WARNING: Appropriate management of complications is possible only when adequate diagnostic and treatment facilities are readily available. Anaphylaxis and severe hypersensitivity reactions characterized by dyspnea and hypotention requiring treatment, angioedema, and generalized urticaria have occurred in 2-4% of patients receiving Taxol in clinical trials. Fatal reactions have occurred in patients despite premedication. All patients should be pre-treated with corticosteroids, diphenhydramine and H_2 antagonists.

THERESA
The drugs are working so well
when they get through attacking my cancer
they attack me.
That's what the doctor says.
Did I tell you I got a part-time job teaching art?
It's a godsend. No benefits, of course,
and not much money,
but now I have something to get up for.

CHORUS
If I didn't have to get out of bed and get dressed.

If I didn't have to look halfway decent.

If there wasn't someplace I had to be
whether I wanted to or not.

I don't think I could get through it.

THERESA
Chemo costs four thousand dollars
a treatment.
I'm supposed
to have six of them.
It's almost funny.
Unbelievable.
I didn't even make
$24,000 last year.

REPORTER
What ever happened to the girl?
The one who wrote everything down
because she couldn't talk?

THERESA
I never saw her again.

REPORTER
Oh.
Umm.
So,
how
are
you
doing?

THERESA
I was so nervous Wednesday

about paying for more chemo
I just broke down.
I bought a fishing license and some worms.
I sat in a pretty stiff wind at the lake trying to pretend
I was somebody else.
I actually caught three bass!

That made me feel better.
Then yesterday, I filled out papers
to get some help paying for the chemo drugs,
and the doctor said he wants me
to just go home and heal for a month.

Hooray! Four weeks without chemo!

My friends Nancy and Beverly had me over for beans and cornbread
and Jello to celebrate.

REPORTER
Anything else good going on?

THERESA
My hair's coming back!

CHORUS
Friday she comes in and tells us she's leaving the hat home
as of Monday and we better be prepared
when she comes to class just her and her bare head.
It's hard not to stare at the stubble.
Very white.
Very short.
An inch.
Maybe two.

What's there is stubborn. Defiant.
A field of white daffodils under a new moon.

THERESA
No more hats.
No more scarves.

REPORTER
Are you dreaming at all these days?

THERESA
Didn't I tell you?
I'm in the beauty parlor all the time.
I'm getting my hair styled
and it's really, really long.

But I wake up in the morning
and I look in the mirror
and I'm shocked
because I think,
"What happened to all my hair?"
And then I remember.
Oh, it was just a dream.
So just beauty parlor dreams
right now.

PAT

Do you think there's a chance
Theresa and I could meet?
Maybe you could bring her here.
She sounds like such a nice person
in the articles.

You know my doctor said the word
at my last appointment. Remission.
I never thought he'd say such a thing,
but that's what my tests show.
He would never say "cured"
but remission is okay by me.

My church group is having a luncheon
in my honor. I hope you can come.
I want to thank everyone
who has been a help,
and you've helped me because
you gave me the chance to help
someone who was worse off than me.

Pat—*pc65@apex.net*

REPORTER

I'll be at the luncheon.
Thank you.
I've told Theresa about you.
When she's feeling better,
she'd like to get together.

THERESA

I found out yesterday
I have six more months of chemotherapy.
In pill form. New pills. Every three weeks.

It's amazing to see how far
treatments have come
in the past three years

but it's still not easy.
People tell me I don't look like
I have cancer.
I get dressed and put on makeup
and I think I look pretty good.

REPORTER
How do you stay in such good spirits?

THERESA
I'm talking to a counselor.
My ex has a girlfriend.
It's another trauma for me.
When he left he said he couldn't take it again,
like he was the one with cancer.

He's been bald for years,
by the way. I got used to that.
Why couldn't he…

But I need to get my head on straight.

Yeah. The bills are piling up again.

It costs thousands.
It's so much
I can't grasp it.

I did get approved for assistance with the new drugs though.
If the drug companies didn't have these programs,
I don't know what I'd do.
It's a comfort to know there's help out there.

Sometimes I feel pain.
That worries me.
My back. My liver.

But if I don't have very long to live,
I want to get rid of some of these ghosts.
That's why I'm going to counseling.

REPORTER
How are you feeling?

THERESA
Honestly?
If I didn't have an IRA,
I'd be eligible for more assistance.
So I was stupid to plan

for the future.
I go to the hospital
and first thing they ask
is if I have insurance.
I look at my hands and feel stupid.
I can still see where all
the skin peeled off.
My back never stops hurting.
I'm afraid I'll cry, but I just
bite my bottom lip
and feel stupid.

The hospital's working with me though,
and that's good. Now I have
a monthly payment plan.
And I'm going to teach as long as I can
because I love it.

REPORTER

What is the doctor saying
these days?

THERESA

They tell me it's gone
to my lymph system.
But that's not so bad,
'cause everywhere the cancer goes,
the chemo goes too.

CHORUS

Cancer's like that. When things get too hot
it hops a boxcar to get out of town.
It lives under bridges with other thugs and roustabouts.
On cold nights they light fires in a barrel,
cluster around it, rubbing
their hands, telling
stories, stealing
whatever's not
nailed down.

REPORTER

Hey, Theresa.
The time is flying by
and I've been away a lot
since our last interview.

How's everything with you?

THERESA
It's hard, my family
being so far away.

Except for my mother.

I think the threat of her
coming to take care of me
is what keeps me
alive.

Guess what?
My tumor markers are down,
so the doctor decided
to stop treatments for awhile longer.
I have to keep on with blood tests
and checkups,
but I'm going to enjoy the time off
if it kills me.

REPORTER
I have some money for you.
The Theresa Fund is growing.

THERESA
Oh, good. I've sold everything to pay the bills.
Cashed in the IRA.
I have so much less than I've ever had in my whole life,
but I have a hard time accepting
that people want to give me money.
I always managed to pay my own way before.
My brother said he would take care of me
if there's ever going to be a time
when I'm refused treatment,
or if I have to take less treatment
because I don't have enough money.
I feel real, real grateful for all that,
but sad at the same time.

The last thing I want to do
is to be a burden to my family.

How amazing about the Theresa Fund.
Could you send me Pat's address?
I want to write her a note. She was the one
who got it all started.

When I get back on my feet
and start making money again

I'll help as many people as I can.
I would like to start making money
that I didn't have to pay to hospitals.
My own money.

CHORUS

Pin money.
Mad money.
Money for a rainy day.

Act IV—The Other Shoe

THERESA
I almost forgot
how great it feels to be well.
I don't take even one day for granted.
I wake up and think, "This is fantastic!
This is just great!" And I'm outdoing myself
to eat right, and exercise and rest.
I had a terrific summer.

REPORTER
—And the doctors?

THERESA
I guess they did too.
But the blood work says
the tumor marker level is up again.
I was hoping
I was in remission.
I really wanted to believe that.
It's fine to believe that.
I'm still very positive that everything's
going to come out ok.
I've got to be positive.

REPORTER
What does the doctor say?

THERESA
If it was two or three points
he wouldn't worry about it,
but now it's more than thirty.
He got me started on something new.

CHORUS
Ten pills every day for fourteen days.

REPORTER
How's it working?

THERESA
About nine hours after I take a full dose
I start feeling kind of woozy.
Not so good.
But people from my church come to help me.

REPORTER

So tell me what you're doing here.

CHORUS

Little bit of painting.

Little bit of carpentry.

Little bit of everything.

We all showed up
to help Theresa out.

REPORTER

And what was your job today?

CHORUS

I came to chop onions and stir the bean soup
so everyone would have something to eat.

My job was also to make Theresa sit down and rest
and let us do the running instead of her.

REPORTER

Did that work out?

CHORUS

Not really.

THERESA

This group from church.
I can't say enough.
They're the best family
anyone could have.
I can't contribute much money,
so I try to help where I can.
I taught vacation bible school this summer.
It was a real fun time.

REPORTER

So it's back to chemo?

THERESA

I'm on a new drug.
But the patient assistance
I had doesn't apply
to this one.

REPORTER
So what are you going to do?

THERESA
Everyone says, "Well,
go on disability. Get some
of that government money."
But I have to stop working to do that,
and to me that's like giving up.

REPORTER
How are you managing with your bills?

THERESA
It's scary.
I've had to put so much on my credit cards.
Some of my medical expenses.
The biggest ones.

And then my truck broke down.
Now with this new chemo
and not getting assistance to pay for the drugs,
that's just turned my world upside down again.
But I can't afford to wait any longer for the medicine
I need.

REPORTER
So how are you—?

THERESA
A friend of mine in town
owns a pharmacy.
They ordered the drugs for me
and got them in. They said
I could start on the treatment
and we could figure out later how I'll pay them.
They didn't want me to wait either.
Thank God.
Not everyone's that fortunate.

REPORTER
Not everyone's that patient about getting paid.

THERESA
Yeah.
But the longer it goes on
the scarier it gets.
I wonder how long I can continue
to take chemo. But the doctor said,

"Well, more is definitely better than less."
So if I'm still around and still able to take chemo,
that's a really good thing.
It's helped me every time.
The longer I stay on chemo,
the closer they are to a cure.
So I'm lucky.
But it's a scary thing.

REPORTER
What's it like living out here
all by yourself?

THERESA
You don't know how your body is going to react
when you start a new treatment.
So being alone is another kind of a scary thing.
I got pretty sick the other night,
here by myself. It was right
in the middle of the night,
but I made it through.
Sometimes you just don't know.

REPORTER
So. Any dreams?

THERESA
Oh, gosh.
My girlfriend was so anxious to find out
if I made it through my second night
of the new chemo, and I was just totally sound asleep
and I was having this dream.

I was in this great big complex of shops
that sold different art materials and gifts
and unusual clothing and other items.

All handmade.

And I was just walking through and thinking,
"How pretty."

I couldn't afford any of it,
but I was just enjoying it all.

And I was supposed to be meeting some friends,
but I couldn't find anybody.
And then I couldn't find my truck.

I was lost
and it was getting dark.

And then someone tapped me
on the shoulder.

I turned around
and saw this angel with a great big
pink fluffy sweater on,
pink chenille.

And she crooked her finger at me,
like come on. Follow me.

So I went with her up this hill
and there was this big warehouse with stained glass windows.
All these people had great big pieces of cloth spread out on the floor
and they were painting. The idea was to take a roller
and make your own pictures.
So I was just beginning to paint and thinking,
"This has got some possibilities…"

And then the phone rang and it was my friend,
seeing if I made it through the night.

REPORTER
So you got what you needed.

THERESA
Yeah. What I like best,
is when you think positively
there are people along the way
to help you find your way
through the confusion.
Just like my friends,
and the pharmacist.

I never thought I would get help like this.
I never expected it. I was so amazed
when the pharmacist's wife called
to say her husband
had ordered the medicine.

CHORUS
It will be here tomorrow
and you can start taking it.

THERESA
I just felt like that

was a miracle.
There are people along the way
who say, "Come this way.
There are ways
through all this."

You just have to keep believing positively
and really miraculous things can develop.
Your way becomes clear.

Act V—Otherwise

PAT

I'm so excited,
but I don't want to say too much
to my family. There's a research study
in Nashville for Parkinsons.
I called them up.
I have an appointment.
My son said he'd drive me.
It would be a miracle
if I could stop this shaking.
Wish me luck.

Pat—pc65@apex.net

REPORTER

So how did it go?
I'm dying to hear.
Oh, God, how stupid.
How did it go?
Let me know.
No. How did it go?
Let me know when you get a chance.
P-l-e-a-s-e
let me know.
I'd appreciate it.
I'd be grateful to hear.
That's it.
I'm keeping my fingers crossed.

PAT

They said I can't be part of the study.
I have dementia.
They gave me one of those memory tests
and I was so nervous I couldn't remember anything.
I just sat in the chair and cried. I never do that.
My son didn't even stand up for me. He knows
I don't have dementia.

Pat—pc65@apex.net

REPORTER
Aren't you angry? Why would they say something like that?
Anyone who spends time with you knows
you're not senile.
It makes me so mad
I want to go down there
and show them your poetry.
And all these emails.

PAT
I'm so relieved to hear you say that.
It got me down for awhile.
A couple of weeks.
And now I'm sick again.
I'm going in for surgery today.
The surgeon is putting a tube in my stomach
so I won't vomit all the time.
It may not work.
Life is hard to give up while my mind and body
are still able to tool around a little.
I told my son when I am unconscious
no more artificial feeding.
I guess, like Paul Harvey,
this is the rest of the story.
Physically anyway.
Spiritually, mentally, emotionally, I'm in tip-top shape.
I'm ready for the real "rest of the story."
The place where faith comes in.
I'm ready for that.
I would still like to meet Theresa.
Is she up to it?
I want you to know, I count you as a friend.
It looks like my time is short.
At least that's what my doctors are saying.
I can't deny it.
Thanks for being a friend.
Closing with my latest poetic effort.

Pat—*pc65@apex.net*

CHORUS

I remember a house.
White with latticed edges
and trimmed with trellised roses.
I think I see a cherry tree
along the side.
Was there an apple tree in back?
Is that a garden there?
If not, I will plant them myself,
where memory finds the scent
of blossom and fruit.
I see him in the doorway,
arms wrapped around a basket
of apples, a cigar in one hand
and a big grin on his face.
The cigar smells sweet.
It was not so long ago
we read the Sunday funnies and laughed.
I look for him still,
and when I see red cherries
and apples and lace curtains
swelling in the fluent breeze,
I know I'll find the way back home
to that old house of ours.

REPORTER

I still haven't told Theresa that Pat died,
but she never asks about her anymore either.
This end of life project is officially over now.
The funding has run out and I have to go on to something new.
But I have boxes of files.
Transcripts from scores of interviews.
I have these stories. These voices.
Some people tell me I should write a book about it.
Others say it's all too depressing and wonder what's wrong with me.

CHORUS

Write a comedy. A musical.
What's wrong with something light
for a change?

REPORTER

They want to know if I've changed,

37

doing all this death-and-dying stuff.

CHORUS
And you say—?

REPORTER
I finally changed the beneficiary on my life insurance
so my first husband won't get a penny.
I have a living will.
And when I die—note that I said "when" not "if"—
I'm going to be cremated and have the ashes scattered
off the Brooklyn Bridge.
My funeral service is planned.
Right down to the music.
Including the whole album of
Sergeant Pepper's Lonely Hearts Club Band.
I'd tell you more, but I'm out of time.
I have to go get Theresa.
She's at chemo today
and she needs a way home.

www.ingramcontent.com/pod-product-compliance
Lightning Source LLC
LaVergne TN
LVHW041558070426
835507LV00011B/1165